P9-CEZ-693

Star in the East

Star in the East

by Hans Holzer

Illustrations by Catherine Buxhoeveden

Harper & Row, Publishers New York, Evanston and London

FIRST EDITION

LIBRARY OF CONGRESS CATALOG CARD NUMBER: 68-29564

I-S

To all men of goodwill
and to those
who are still seeking
the way to the light
I dedicate this book
in the hope that it will
remain in their thoughts
and enter their hearts
so that they may experience
the spirit of Christmas
and always look, with faith,
for their own
Star in the East

Contents

Illustrations

Preface

I HAD always wanted to be a writer and an archaeologist, and by the time I reached the age of eighteen I was both. My college training included history and archaeology as well as journalism, and I was real proud when my very first article on eighteenth-century art was accepted by a local newspaper.

That was the beginning of a long quest in which my search for little known or completely new facts in history and science became a mission in life. Let others repeat what already exists, I thought, I want to be a real digger and come up with the unusual, the unknown, the startling: as a numismatist and coin collector, I specialized in unpublished coins, so that I could publish them. I liked to try my hand at digs others had given up or pronounced hopeless. When my optimistic outlook turned up some unusual objects, nevertheless, the joy of discovery was twice as great.

I think we do our best work when we consider our

job a pleasure. So it was with me: studying the artifacts of the past wasn't work at all. It was a reward by Fate for the unusual interest I had shown as a student in this field, while other young people turned to the more conventional pursuits of medicine or law.

I soon learned that ancient civilizations weren't the dry, two-dimensional worlds of some history books. Far from it. As I read the secondary sources in Roman, Greek, and Egyptian history, I discovered new perspectives. The people who were the pivotal forces in these worlds were as human and three-dimensional as we are, they acted pretty much as people always did and still do, and nothing was really black and white, heroic or mean, but a little of both.

My curiosity concerning the ancient worlds gradually zeroed in on Palestine, the excitement of this cradle of civilization somehow attracting me even more than Greece or Egypt. Although I am basically pantheistic in my religious outlook, I have always been fascinated by the beauty of ecclesiastical ritual and have often wondered how much of it is based upon historical evidence.

Thus it happened that during my formative years a mounting interest in the Bible intermingled with my archaeological studies. Whenever I picked up a coin of ancient Judaea, ripples of excitement ran through my fingers at the thought that I might be touching the very same widow's mite Jesus had held. As a writer, I of course had a generous amount of imagination, all the more reason not to allow it to take the place of hard facts. Not, that is, if I wanted to be taken seriously. My initial efforts in this field were published by some of the scholarly magazines that tolerated no nonsense. You either had the facts or you didn't get any space.

Throughout my long years of college, both at Columbia in New York and at Vienna University in Austria, I puzzled over the narratives of the Bible. More especially did I wonder about the birth of Jesus and the two most moving reports that followed this event: the experiences of the shepherds in the hills of Judaea and the journey of the Wisemen from parts unknown to worship the Christ child.

There were those around me who would smile benignly whenever I cautiously remarked that perhaps some of the Biblical events actually had occurred. For I grew up in a time when it was fashionable to think that religion was a fable. It did not sway me, as I had an inner conviction that my hunch could someday, somehow, be proven right.

But the pressures of life, the necessity of earning a living—as a writer and editor—managed to relegate these urgings to the background. Meanwhile, whenever I had a constructive thought on how to prove some of the Christmas story as factual, I would jot it down and file it away for later use.

Over the years, that file grew and grew until it burst at the seams and I could ignore it no longer. One day I pulled it out accidentally and my interest grew again. Tomorrow I would start work on a book about the Wisemen and the Star of Bethlehem! Alas, the morrow brought other news: dark clouds on the political horizon.

Within weeks I was on my way to New York where

my father had spent many years of his adolescence. The Biblical research folder had come along with me, of course, but the requirements of adjusting to a different life and a new home came first.

Whenever I heard someone at Christmas time speak of Peace on Earth, I felt a nudge within me to contribute to that Peace that was yet to come by writing my book.

And then I did.

Star in the East

1

Christmas On Long Island

IT WAS EARLY morning when I walked down the steps leading from the little church on Long Island to the street below. It was quite an ordinary church, not very old, not very outstanding, but very full this night. The Christmas service, the Midnight Mass, had just been celebrated and there was solemnity in the air as well as that undefineable extra something we call, for want of a better word, the spirit of Christmas.

I was a young man and religion in the formal sense meant little to me, but the adventure of a Christmas service had attracted me and I wanted to be among people on this night. I was still single and rather lonely and there was something warm and friendly in the community of a similar festive purpose which had united the people for an hour or so on this ice-cold December night.

As I sauntered down the street, a man's voice broke through the silence in back of me. There was some snow on the ground, as befits the season, and the voice sounded muffled.

"That was a nice service, wasn't it?" he said, and as I looked around, the man came up beside me. He was all bundled up in a dark coat and woolen scarf, but his face stuck out and I could see he was about my age.

I merely nodded and my eyes wandered up to the sky. We both stopped, for you can't walk very fast with your eyes on the stars. But the spectacle up there was far more interesting than anything we could possibly see on the ground at this hour. The firmament, literally blanketed with stars of all sizes, sparkled and put on a grand display. There were shooting stars too and I did not fail to make a quick wish as they shot out of sight.

After a while we moved on. For a moment I did not say anything. But my companion had said something a few minutes earlier, and it deserved an answer, even if belated.

"Yes, it was an impressive service," I said, nodding again. "So many people stayed up for it, too."

The man at my side shrugged under his heavy overcoat.

"Curiosity probably for most. It's quite a show, you know."

We halted again.

"Don't you think," I said, "that religious beliefs had anything to do with their coming?"

What sort of fellow was my new acquaintance? A cynic perhaps?

I moved along.

"Oh, I don't doubt that they're all good church-going folk," he said, and continued to walk, strangely enough, in my direction, so I could not very well shake him, if I had wanted to.

"But I wonder how many of them really believe," he went on, "I mean really way deep down inside."

I wondered myself.

Did I believe? Did I come here because I was convinced that Jesus the Christ was born at this hour, almost two thousand years ago? I did not. I came because I loved the spirit of the Christmas celebration. That was the important thing. Not statistics.

"You're absolutely right," my companion said as we walked across the broad boulevard, quite deserted at this hour, "it's the spirit that counts."

I was cheered by the thought that we were in agreement and kept silent for a few moments, until it occurred to me that I had not said anything aloud. Had my companion read my thoughts?

I looked at him from the side, but he seemed just like any other ordinary fellow one might meet at a church service. There was nothing ethereal or unusual about him. And yet, he made me feel uncomfortable.

"What about you? Do you believe?"

Christmas on Long Island

"Believe in what?" he shot back and kept walking.

"Believe in a literal Christmas, I mean, the story of the birth, the Jesus child, the Holy Family—the works?"

He chuckled at my directness.

"Is believing so important?" he asked. "Belief is the uncritical acceptance of something you either cannot or do not wish to prove scientifically," he added.

I knew what he meant. I'd often been asked by people who knew of my firm convictions of the reality of extrasensory perception, whether I really believed in the psychic world.

Belief did not enter the picture at all, of course. Facts are not subject to the courtesy of belief. They're there, take them or leave them, but facts don't play favorites and their reality is assured regardless of your attitude toward them. That's why, to me at least, to be scientific is to be factual.

My new-found friend had the same attitude toward believing as I had, and that pleased me, of course, but it occurred to me that he had not yet answered my question about the *story* of the Bible.

Was he avoiding the issue? Did he feel embarrassed?

"Not at all," he said, again reading my innermost thoughts. "I'm coming to that. I don't believe in believing, as such, but I am sure that the Nativity is of the greatest spiritual and moral significance for mankind. It does not matter whether it really happened or not."

I was somewhat surprised at his cynical attitude. Doesn't matter?

"Exactly," he repeated, "because it is a symbol to millions of people, a symbol of God's presence, through Jesus, in all of us."

"Now wait a moment," I heard myself say, "it isn't as simple as that. It matters a great deal whether or not there was a Jesus Chirst, whether he was born in Bethlehem and whether or not the adoration of the shepherds took place. These are cornerstones of the Christian faith. Bulwarks of religion. Without them, you have doubt. Doubt that anything at all in the Bible is true. Isn't that so?"

But my young friend shook his head underneath the hat he had pressed down on his forehead as protection against the cold wind which rose a bit more as the night wore on.

We were now not too far from my house and I began to wonder where my companion lived. Probably one of the newer developments just beyond, I figured, and realized that we would soon be parted. I was thankful to him for his companionship, for he made the icy walk home cheerful and his conversation with me shortened the time for both of us.

"To those who accept the spiritual meaning of Christmas," he finally said, "the Biblical facts themselves are always secondary. If you were to prove tomorrow that Christmas never happened, it would not matter to them, as their own, private Christmas was always celebrated in their hearts. But they are a small minority and their faith is like a beleaguered fortress amid hordes of selfish people."

"Quite," I said. I agreed with him, but I could

not let him get away without an answer to my last statement.

"If we can prove that the Bible is true, I mean that these people really existed, wouldn't it make a lot of difference to those who look on it as a fable?"

He thought for a while.

"I suppose you're right," he admitted, "but it would have to be scientific proof."

"Of course," I readily agreed, "but will you give me your definition of what scientific evidence consists of?"

My companion pulled his scarf, which had come loose, a bit tighter as we started to approach my block.

I deliberately slowed down, for I wanted to hear his definition before it was time to say good-night.

He slowed down too and cleared his throat, thereby sending up clouds of steam into the still night air.

"The word 'science,'" he finally said, "is derived from the Latin and means to find out or to obtain knowledge and thus know. Scientific evidence is not subject to opinion, interpretation, philosophies, points of view, and such. Only the deductions arrived at after obtaining the scientific evidence may be interpreted. Don't confuse opinion with fact."

"Never," I promised. "But after I have my facts straight, can I have an opinion?"

"Absolutely," he agreed. "In fact, you must. Without an opinion based on your scientific findings, the whole job won't be worth doing. Difference is, now your opinions have substance, solid evidence to back you up."

I was glad we agreed on practically everything now.

"Then you don't think it is wrong to try to prove the Bible, do you? I mean if someone could." The question just came to my mind.

"Not at all," he assured me, and expansively waved an arm toward the sky.

"God created all this, too, and man is trying to explore it. Why not God's own book? If it will make better men?"

Of that I wasn't sure, but it certainly could not make worse men. Mankind was pretty low as it stood. No place to go but up, I thought.

I was in front of my house now and it was bitter cold. Before I went inside, there was one more question I wanted to ask my companion.

"All those people we saw tonight, in church," I said, "how many of them do you think believe in Christmas as a concrete fact?"

"A few," he admitted.

"How can you know?"

"I know. I spoke to them. I heard them. I know."

"Not many?"

"Not many, no. A few."

"And if someone gave them hard, solid facts about Christmas, would it change their reluctance to accept Christmas as real?"

"It might."

My friend was becoming monosyllabic, probably because of the intense cold around us, and I really had no right to keep him from going home.

"Then it's worth doing, isn't it?" I said, and waited for his reply.

I could not help glancing up at the firmament again for a moment of reassurance.

I looked in his direction.

He was gone, and the wide expanse of snow-covered street around me was quite empty.

I suddenly realized I had been talking to myself.

2

What Exactly is Christmas?

I DECIDED to start all over, but to start with the obvious. What was Christmas, what did it mean to various people in various countries and at different times? I had learned long ago that traditions are always based on a kernel of truth and that one must never discard without careful examination what might be conceived of as fictional or the product of folklore alone.

I am indebted to Marion Todd, who edited a Christmas book some years ago, for the information that the first North American Christmas celebration took place in 1619 at Jamestown, Virginia. The early American festivities centered on the good things of life: food, drink, and merrymaking in a world of strangers and dangers. Drawing from the traditions of the European lands they had left, the early Americans naturally followed the customs of the old country. Holly and mistletoe, English in origin, the Christmas log, of Scandinavian background, and the tradition of St. Nicholas, which came to America by way of Holland, all made the early celebrations a mixture of various traditions.

The first legal Christmas observance in New England took place in 1686 at the Governor's house in Boston, but Christmas did not become a legal holiday in the Bay area until the middle of the nineteenth century. The decorating of streets, even of entire towns, is decidedly popular to this day in the northeast of the United States, as are wooden crèches and even live re-enactments of the nativity scene in churches. Carol singing, a decidedly English custom, also still flourishes in New England.

The twentieth century made Christmas more and more into a social and commercial occasion, gradually lessening its religious and mystic implications.

Endless rounds of parties start off the week of Christmas, and anyone still entirely sober at the time of the holiday itself is hardly worth his salt. Christmas is an excuse to suspend the normal routine, the bleak working day for some, the boring sameness of security for others, to engage in a bit of horseplay and empty conversation with people one would scarcely notice were it not for the ever-present and totally abused "Christmas spirit."

It is unfortunate that most of the American Christmas spirit comes in bottles and only a minority of people celebrate the holiday with some semblance of religious feelings.

There is nothing wrong with the idea of exchanging gifts. As long as the gifts were modest and intensely personal, and were brought along to the Christmas feast by the donor himself, the custom had charm and meaning. But the nature of gifts in America has changed. Suitable gifts of the past, such as candy, flowers, jewelry, or toys for the children are now not so popular as liquor, cars, fur coats, and the ever-present cash payment. No longer are toys mainly of animals, dolls, and other representations of daily life. Rather are they of instruments of destruction, such as tanks, guns, and bombs, hardly in keeping with the festival honoring the "Prince of Peace."

Christmas habits in America have been so corrupted as to obscure the original intent. Only man's eternal greed, superficially concealed by a false and noisy "spirit of the occasion," remains. America, however, is not alone in this sad triumph of materialism; Europe and the rest of the civilized world have also succumbed to it.

Happily, there is everywhere a quiet, somewhat embarrassed minority of individuals who still hold to a more meaningful "old-fashioned Christmas." Their voices are not overloud, except, of course, in their own hearts.

I took a good look at the European traditions of Christmas and discovered that several entirely different and separate holidays had been merged into one to create today's tradition.

It did not start with the birth of Jesus at all, I soon found out, but with the ancient pre-Christian festival of the winter solstice. I do not use the word "pagan" as did the early Christians to denote all those who did not believe in *their* religion. In the first place, the word, literally, only means "of the country" as opposed to the more sophisticated world of the city and advanced civilizations. But I am also firmly convinced that the non-Christians were not necessarily inferior in their religious beliefs to the Christians; in fact, they are still not the less inspired, except that they differ in their *approach* to God. Certainly, the moral fibers of Islam, Judaism, and Buddhism, to name the world's other principal religions, are as high as those of the Christian traditions.

Thus, long even before Judaism became a power in the Mediterranean world, the people of Western Europe lived by a religion commonly called "The Old Religion," which today's followers—and there are many who still live by this Celtic-Germanic tradition—call witchcraft. It has nothing to do with magic or the imaginary world of medieval witchery, invented by a jealous church to blacken the vestiges of the remaining "pagans." No witch rides a broom or cackles over a black cat familiar. But the Druidic priests of England, Ireland, Scotland, and France celebrated the holiday of the solstice in a worthy and emotionally satisfying manner at least as beautiful as the Christmas celebration.

To this day, the English-speaking countries have a Christmas-at-home celebration, usually a week before the holiday, in which the "hanging of the greens" and the "wassail ceremony" are remnants of ancient pre-Christian rituals. The greens of course stem from the Druidic groves and signify the eternal aspects of life. The word "wassail" is of Norse origin and roughly corresponds to the toast "To your health!" The wassail bowl contains the punch, with which today's celebrants usher in the Christmas period. The old Norsemen used far stronger stuff.

The Boar's Head dinners are no longer serving actual boars, but have mostly replaced this ferocious animal with something gentler and easier to catch. But in Merrie Auld England boars still represented a menace and were hunted down by the gentry and citizens alike. In a way then, serving the boar's head in prominent position signifies man's conquest of the wild elements around him.

Although Christmas is a religious holiday, the celebration of it in the English-speaking countries was very worldly indeed until quite recently, when a resurgence of spiritual meaning at least kept pace with the physical aspects of the feast. Excesses in food, drink, and love-making were part and parcel of the holiday "spirit."

This was a far cry from the simple and venerable approach to the holiday practiced by "The Old Religion." In solemn procession, the white-gowned priests went to the sacred groves where they worshiped an invisible deity among the oak trees that symbolized his powers. Their church had no roof except the sky above. Wearing sprigs of holly in their hair, the priests then proceeded to cut the mistletoe found in the trees. This plant was a symbol of fertility and power to them, but on a more practical level—and all religions have such a level—it was an excellent antidote against poison and was extensively used in ancient medicine.

The holly tree, incidentally, because of its evergreen nature, symbolized life eternal to them, and it is true that even today's "white witches" are firmly convinced that reincarnation is the way of life. Since Christianity also accepts life eternal as a fact, the holly tradition was transferred into the new religion without qualms.

But the fact remains that the use of any forms of greens in the Christmas service is entirely pre-Christian and has nothing to do with the nativity.

The Druids sang chants to create a harmonious atmosphere among the celebrants, although the Druidic solstice festival was a serious and somber affair not at all like the gay Christmas celebration of today. The chants also entered into the Christian traditions and became the caroling, the singing of songs of the season, probably one of the nicer traditions still being practiced in our day. The record industry has seen fit to jump on the bandwagon with Christmas "songs" hardly fit for the occasion, but the carols are still being heard where the phonograph is silent.

In ancient Rome, the festival of the *Saturnalia*,

honoring the agricultural deity Saturn, also took place during the winter solstice at the end of December. However, Saturn's original position was that of God-father, long before the Greek Zeus-Jupiter pushed him off his celestial throne. The Saturnalia were thus also festivals of renewal, marking the dying year and the hope for a new spring. But since they often ended in merrymaking of a carnal kind, they were hardly of a higher religious connotation. Neither, of course, were the huge quantities of food and drink consumed as a symbol of Christmas in medieval Europe.

In the Anglo-Saxon world, the Christ child is of minor importance. Only in recent years has Father Christmas, a copy of the Central European Santa Claus, become a fixture in the English-Christmas pantheon. The crèche is essentially a Catholic prerogative, and it is in Ireland where we find today the strongest religious connotations of Christmas in Europe.

There, hymn singing and candle lighting are intensely religious in nature and fervor and the devout are perhaps most primitive and direct in their relationship to the Christmas story.

In Germany, the religious aspects of the festival center around the Holy Night, December 24, when the Midnight Mass, and in the villages especially, Christmas trumpeting, herald the birth of the babe. Both the 25th and 26th of December are either legal or traditional holidays and nobody goes to work on those days.

In Germany and Austria, the Christmas tree had a particularly early and strong foothold as part of the yuletide festival. Bringing the tall tree of "The

Old Religion" indoors and dressing it with lights and other glitter really stems from pre-Christian times. However, the tree ceremony is Scandinavian rather than Celtic.

Another custom still prevalent in some areas is the feeling that the Christmas night may bring to unmarried women prophecies about their future. It probably relates to the New Year's Eve custom of throwing molten lead into hot water and interpreting the resulting odd shapes in the manner a tea-leaf reader interprets the leaves in the cup.

Although today's Christmas celebrations center around the assumed date of the nativity, December 24 in the United States and England, this is not so in other countries. In America, Santa Claus conveniently arrives on Christmas Eve, but it is never quite explained how he relates to the Christ child, the shepherds, and the three Kings.

I was, of course, wondering if Virginia wasn't right and there was indeed a Santa Claus.

Some years ago I stood in a rather mawkish-looking church in Bari, Southern Italy, in front of the tomb of St. Nicholas. As a child I had "met" Santa Claus in kindergarten from age three on. This *Nicolo*, as he is called in Austria in the Italian manner, did not come alone. He had with him a sinister-looking fellow called *Krampus*, dressed up as the devil, complete with horns, chains, a fagot to whip bad children with, and a wooden bucket strapped to his back, into which, presumably, the children selected for punishment would be put. St. Nicholas, of course, was a bishop wearing a red soutane, a white beard, and a mitre. He held his shepherd's crook in one hand, using the other to distribute nuts and fruit from a bag.

In Germany, the jolly elf in the red coat is sometimes called *Kriss Kringle*. This is not an attempt to deglamorize the old man, but merely a distortion of the words "Christ Kind," meaning Christ child. The term Kriss Krinkle has also found its way to America where it was last used in a Broadway musical oddly called *Here's Love*. In this Meredith Wilson work, Kriss Kringle was the name a department store Santa Claus used when signing his social security card. His abode was given as the North Pole, where we also find Santa's toyshop. This shop has never been photographed despite repeated flights over the area by several commercial airlines and is mainly the brainchild of Clement Clarke Moore, whose famed poem "A Visit from St. Nicholas" had Santa coming from the North Pole.

Incidentally, Santa Clausing is a regular occupation among unemployed actors during the Christmas season, and those lucky enough to have their own beards are even more in demand. Surely they, if no one else, must believe there is a Santa Claus!

But there really *was* a Santa Claus.

"Claus" is an abbreviation of the Dutch Nicolaus, who was born in the Turkish seaside town of Patara. He was a man from a well-to-do family with a kind disposition toward his fellow man. In fourth-century Asia Minor, this Nicholas is said to have helped an impoverished neighbor with three marriageable daughters but no dowry. Not wanting to hurt the man's pride, Nicholas threw a purse of money through the chimney into the man's house. He had done this sort of thing before, getting pleasure from helping the poor anonymously. The impoverished receiver of the money ascribed his good fortune to God and his incessant prayers, but it turned out that that Nicholas had not put enough money into the purse. Nicholas, who was the Bishop of nearby Myra, repeated the trick with the purse twice more.

Unfortunately, he was caught by the neighbor the third time, but managed to escape.

Word of his deeds got around, however, although the townspeople decided not to talk about it out of respect for Nicholas. That at least is the traditional story of Nicholas' generosity and its consequences. We have no way of checking up on it, but we do know that he was buried at Myra in the year 342 A.D. and that his death occurred on December 6. Myra, which is now called Demre by the Turks, has a Church of St. Nicholas and the original Santa Claus was buried in its crypt.

The place became a shrine and pilgrims from all over the world visited it. In the year 1087, some Italian sailors decided to do better than that. They broke open the marble sarcophagus and stole the bones of the Saint. These bones were then reburied in the Church of St. Nicholas in Bari, which I visited. But the sailors had left a couple of bones behind by accident, so that the original Church of St. Nicholas in Myra also has *part* of the Saint!

The date of December 6, considerably earlier than the nativity, is the day when in Central Europe Santa Claus and his dark companion make the rounds. He does not "come" on Christmas Eve at all. That's another fellow called the Christmas Man or Father Christmas. Admittedly, he looks a lot like Santa, but he is not the Saint who lies buried in two places. Somebody has to hand out the gifts to the children, and the tradition of Father Christmas took care of that in recent times.

About that sinister-looking companion traveling with the Saint: in Central Europe they call him *Krampus*, a word of doubtful origin meaning devil, and December 5 is *his* day. But convenience being what it is, he comes a day later with St. Nicholas. In the Lowlands, incidentally, Santa comes during the night between the 5th and 6th of December, leaving presents, of course, and he is accompanied by a dark-skinned aide and a donkey.

I found that the next date for a celebration tying in with the Christmas season comes December 13 in the Nordic countries. It is the day of St. Lucia, and is based on an alleged vision of this Italian Saint having occurred in Sweden many centuries ago during a period of famine. The tradition demands that a young girl re-enact her appearance, wearing a crown of candles and offering breakfast to anyone lucky enough to be in Scandinavia on that day. St. Lucia helps the poor and hungry and in this manner gradually became associated with the Goodwill Toward Men aspect of Christmas, or Yul, as it is called in the north of Europe. There is also a local version of Santa Claus, called the Julenisse, a cross between the traditional image of Santa Claus and a wood sprite, perhaps a remainder of ancient pre-Christian traditions.

In France, additional emphasis is placed on the last day of the Christmas period, the Epiphany, or Three Kings' Day, or Twelfth Night as it is alternately called. There is a game involving a bean hidden under someone's plate. The one who finds it is the "king" or "queen" of the occasion and all others must do his or her bidding.

In Italy, Santa Claus does not have to work so hard on Christmas Day, lugging presents for the children. He has a helper in the person of an old crone called the *Befana* who does all the work during the night. The name of this mythical helper is derived from the Italian word for Epiphany.

In the Americas, traditional celebrations in addition to the essentially religious aspects center around the *posada* or request for shelter. This refers to the arrival at the inn of Joseph and Mary. In Mexico and Guatemala, *posada* is celebrated for nine days prior to December 24. Each night the actors representing the Holy Couple are refused admission to a different house, but on the final night the woman is admitted as "the queen of heaven."

In time St. Nicholas became associated with the sea as a patron Saint of sailors, and it was in this capacity that he came to North America aboard a Dutch vessel headed for Nieuw Amsterdam. As for the reindeer, Clement Clarke Moore must again be blamed for this charming touch. He did not invent them, but he invented their names and made them a household word, except of course for Rudolph, who came somewhat later and who sold more phonograph records for his creator than any other song ever did, including "Silent Night," which did not earn its author a nickel.

Even Japan, the most un-Christmassy of all countries, has lately hopped on the reindeer "gravy train." Department stores along the Ginza, Tokyo's Broadway, feature the jolly Saint, and there is a 30-foot-tall St. Nick to remind the Japanese that they are now allied with the West whence all Santas come.

Perhaps a more fitting addition to the worldwide celebration of the Christmas period was recently made in the Holy Land itself. In time for Midnight Mass, 1965, a brand new church, the Basilica of the Annunciation, opened its doors to worshipers at Nazareth, Israel. Five years in the building, the church stands on the spot where the Archangel Gabriel traditionally announced the birth of Jesus to Mary, and on which churches have existed since the fourth century. So universal was the appeal of a new Christian church on this spot that it drew craftsmen and materials from many nations. The windows were made in Austria, the church organ in Germany, the sculpture came from Italy, and the workmen were Israelis.

Nazareth, the town where Jesus grew into a man, has always been considered sacred, second only in this respect to Bethlehem itself. The bitterness of two thousand years has disappeared at least in the land where Christ's teachings originated, and the Israeli officials of Nazareth help celebrate the Christmas day as much as any holiday in the Hebrew calendar. This is as it should be, for Christ's foremost teachings concerned love for one's neighbor, forgiveness of sins and errors, and peaceful coexistence with those who had beliefs other than one's own.

The idea of a Savior is by no means unique in religious thought. Although the Hebrews as a purely monotheistic people were able to formulate their thoughts about the hoped-for Messiah better than other nations, the idea is indeed universal.

The Egyptian pantheon bears a remarkable similarity to the Christ tradition. Here too, the son of God dies to save mankind from its sins. Brahma, Buddha, Moses, Mohammed—all the great prophets and religious leaders had much in common with both the teachings and fate of Jesus.

Historically, the world was ready for a religious renewal at the time of Jesus' birth. The Roman Empire was approaching its zenith, the Greek world was dying and a new faith was desperately needed. Had Jesus not been born at this time, perhaps some other great leader might have come along to renew the ancient Hebrew religion and give it the universalism it had lacked.

3

Christmas Traditions and Christmas Facts

I KNEW by now that there was much in the Christmas tradition that was arbitrary and accidental, and certainly not historical in any sense of the word.

The question in my mind was whether any of the nativity itself was factual. I decided to assume that Christ might have been born on a night other than December 24. My approach was to treat the nativity narrative as a purely local Palestinian event and to discard all later additions, interpretations, and possible distortions of the original occurrence.

Joseph and Mary were refused admission at the inn, not too hard to understand at that crowded time of year when a census was taking place and people from many hills and backwoods had come down to be taxed. The fact that she was pregnant and was still refused shelter does not speak well of the innkeeper. But Palestine at that period was seething with rebellion and unrest, and graciousness toward one's fellow men was not so strongly present as it would be in a calmer and happier clime.

We have as yet not discovered the foundations of that inn at Bethlehem, but we may very well find it someday. If Jesus was indeed born in the wooden manger adjacent to the inn, no trace of it would now exist. Humble birth for the Savior of the world would be a natural prerequisite of a new religion and might have been added as a later touch. Against this possibility we do have the testimony of the two Evangelists Matthew and Luke.

Two accounts seemed particularly suitable for possible historical corroboration, the account of the adoration of the shepherds and the arrival of the three Kings. There are a number of old Christmas songs dealing with these subjects, and allowing for the poetic license of the lyricists, one can still learn certain basic traditions from them.

One of the few American carols enjoying widespread popularity is "O Little Town of Bethlehem," the work of Phillips Brooks and Lewis H. Redner, who respectively composed the words and music in 1868. "Hark! the Herald Angels Sing" was written in 1743 by Charles Wesley, brother of the famed minister,

Grotto outside Bethlehem

John Wesley, and later arranged to music composed in 1840 by Felix Mendelssohn-Bartholdy. Following closely the King James rendition of the Gospel according to St. Luke, a line reads "With angelic hosts proclaim, 'Christ is born in Bethlehem.'" The most famous of all carols, "Silent Night," composed in 1818 by Franz Grüber, an Austrian schoolteacher, with words by Joseph Mohr, refers to the adoration with "Shepherds hear the angels sing, 'Alleluia; hail the King!'"

Another old carol is the French "Noel, Noel," rendered into English as "The First Noel." Here the shepherds are described as "keeping their sheep" in the fields "on a cold winter's night" when the event happened. "They looked up and saw a star shining in the east, beyond them far. And to the earth it gave great light, and so it continued both day and night."

Not very likely.

"Hark! the Herald Angels Sing" adds a new dimension to the simple messenger of God: angel, meaning messenger, now becomes a herald as well. A messenger brings news of a private nature. A herald tells all the world.

But Christmas carols need not be religious in nature. "Jingle Bells" captures the spirit of the holiday season with its dashing sleighs. Provided, that is, that you live in a country that can count on a white Christmas.

Even so mundane a song as "Rudolph, the Rednosed Reindeer" can be considered a genuine carol. It uses the same alliterative technique of heaping similar vowels one upon the other to create a brittle and joyful word picture as did the older "Hark! the Herald Angels Sing" for more sedate reasons.

"On the First Day of Christmas" is England's contribution to the seasonal celebration, taking in, as it does, the entire feast right through the Epiphany. And the ballad of Good King Wenceslaus is sung by people who very likely never heard of this old Bohemian king and his festive habits.

Some carols don't even have music. Charles Dickens' justly celebrated story, "A Christmas Carol," and Clement Clarke Moore's "A Visit from St. Nicholas" are true carols in the sense that they, too, tell the story of the Christmas time and spirit.

The Christmas carols can hardly be taken as scientific sources, but it is always interesting to note how poetic license sometimes enlarges upon the original.

Most people know the Bible only as it is usually published, whether it be the King James Version, Roman Catholic version, or the Greek original. The latter was based on the Aramaic version, which was translated into Greek at an early date.

One of the most independent translations is George Ricker Berry's "interlinear" translation, in which the original Greek words are first translated word by word next to the "traditional" version, giving the reader an immediate chance to check up on some glaring differences. This work was first undertaken in 1897 and recently republished by Wilcox & Follett.

But there are chapters left out of the Bible today which may at one time have belonged in it; chapters that contain material far closer to the time of Jesus than some of the material that is now included in the Holy Scriptures.

A short time ago the so-called Dead Sea Scrolls, discovered in a cavern at Qumran in what is now Jordan, reopened the entire question of what is and what is not properly part of the New Testament. The Book of Enoch, for instance, also called the Essenean Bible, may have been written during the lifetime of Jesus. Charles Francis Potter, who has devoted years of study to this work, is convinced that it was authored by Jesus himself. He bases his opinion on certain similarities in the writing with some of the lines attributed to Jesus in the gospels of Luke and Matthew.

The excavations at Qumran are continuing, but already the cavern appears to have been a kind of early Christian seminary. In one cave alone, ten versions of the Book of Enoch were found. Jesus spent many years among the Essenes, a sect teaching a religion similar to early Christianity.

In addition to the esoteric literature known as Pseudepigrapha, of which the Book of Enoch is part, there are also the Apocrypha or "unofficial" gospels, which some, but by no means all, Bibles include.

One of the most cherished traditions, nay, one of the sacred pillars upon which much of the Catholic faith is built, is the Immaculate Conception of Mary. Jesus' supernormal birth has become not only a cornerstone of orthodox religion, but a major subject in the world of art. And yet, Jesus does not refer to this event himself in any part of the Scriptures. It was not a strong concept in the early Christian world. Jesus' reference to "his father," meaning God-Father, was clearly spiritual in meaning, just as his title of "King of the Jews" at no time referred to temporal power. His execution on the trumped-up charges of having assumed this title was a political expediency in which both Pontius Pilate's government and the ruling priests must share blame. It was a politically nervous time and Jesus' martyrdom was the result.

Many religious leaders have been linked with a deity, as have important statesmen. Julius Caesar claimed descent from Venus, and the Japanese mikados, until recently, considered the sun goddess Amaterasu their ancestor. The Dalai Lama is a reincarnated Buddha. China's emperors were always referred to as "Son of Heaven," alluding to their supernatural birth. Greek mythology is full of mortal leaders whose parents were gods.

The link with deities is not to be taken factually; it merely expresses the need for supernormal birth among leaders in ancient and even not so ancient times. It is unlikely that a ruler who does not also dominate the minds of his subjects will long remain powerful in the material world. From this point of view should be understood the moves of Henry VIII in setting up the Church of England, or the Czars heading up the Russian Orthodox Church in the nineteenth century. The Roman Emperor Augustus created the state religion of emperor worship purely as a political means of controlling his people. A state in which a religious leader wields power in opposition to the temporal ruler cannot long endure. The continual strife between the medieval popes and the Holy Roman emperors eventually led to the destruction of that Empire.

The Immaculate Conception thus added the mystery of Divine origin to the moral stature of Christ. He did not need it, for his position was securely established in his own lifetime by virtue of his teachings, his healings, his leadership. Although modern psychic research acknowledges the possibility that the resurrection might have taken place exactly as described and that it is *scientifically* acceptable *on that basis,* we have no scientific basis on which to judge the probability or even the possibility of an Immaculate Conception.

Had this been an established fact during the lifetime of Jesus, much more would have been made of it in the Scriptures, but the propagation of this event is mainly medieval and follows the events of Jesus' birth by several, if not indeed many, centuries.

There were other wondrous events surrounding the birth of the Christ far more capable of verification than the Immaculate Conception, and I decided to direct my efforts into such channels as might yield the best results, scientifically speaking.

4

The Adoration of The Shepherds

THROUGHOUT the past nineteen hundred years, artists have been impressed by the two themes glorifying the birth of the Christ child: the adoration of the shepherds and the visit of the three Kings. These events have been represented on canvas, in stone, on wood, even on silver and gold coins, and though the traditional event is always kept more or less as it is described in the New Testament, the faces, expressions, and raiments of the configurants are mostly those of the time in which the artist worked. Thus we have some very curious Kings attending the babe, looking more like sixteenth-century warriors than ancient potentates.

A painter is free to represent his subjects symbolically, of course, and his use of live models for the figures makes this the more sensible. What puzzled me at first was the source of these "traditional" events. How far back could we trace the traditions? I did not expect to find an unbroken link between antiquity and the present, but I did hope that somewhere I might discover something in addition to the well-known—and well-worn—narratives of Matthew and Luke.

The *Adoration of the Shepherds,* of course, came first, even though today in many churches the crèche shows the shepherds inside the manger, with the three Kings waiting in the wings. This is probably for the convenience of the audience, because there is evidence to show that the shepherds and the Kings not only never met, but were apart in terms of time and perhaps even space.

The original mention of the story about the shepherds and the appearance of what is generally termed "the Star of Bethlehem" is in the Gospel according to St. Luke, Chapter 2. Luke tells of how the shepherds in the hills around Bethlehem were going about their business, watching their flocks, when "the angel of the Lord came upon them, and the glory of the Lord *shone* round about them," as the King James Version puts it.

Naturally, being simple and somewhat superstitious people, they were afraid of what they considered a supernormal phenomenon. We shall examine the nature of the light that "shone round about them" presently.

Bethlehem

The angel, Luke reports, went on to calm their fears and to tell them of the birth of the Savior in nearby Bethlehem, advising them where they could find the babe. The King James Version continues:

"And suddenly there was with the angel a multitude of the heavenly host praising God, and saying, Glory to God in the highest, and on earth peace, good will toward men. And it came to pass, as the angels were gone away from them into heaven, the shepherds said one to another, Let us now go even unto Bethlehem."

Curiously, neither Matthew nor Mark mentions this event, so we have only the Greek physician's testimony that it happened.

According to Luke, the Shepherds saw a light, which turned out to be an angel, and suddenly there was with the angel "a multitude of the heavenly host." I wonder how many people understand what a heavenly host means.

To me, the words *"egeneto . . . plethos stratias ouraniou,"* in the original Greek text, only mean "there appeared a big light." Dr. Berry gives *"egeneto"* as "there was produced," *"plethos"* as "plenty," and *"stratias ouraniou"* as "stars of the sky," just as it occurs elsewhere, in Acts 7, as *"stratia tou ouranou,"* referring to the stars, for the Jews were punished not for worshiping "the host of heaven," but "the stars in heaven"! Luke's rendition thus has been changed from a factual "there appeared a big star" into something quite different and far less plausible—"a multitude of the heavenly host."

Luke's account in the common translation in general use today, continues with "praising God, and saying

. . . ," making it appear as if the heavenly host were praising God. However, the original Greek construction suggests to me that Luke said *the shepherds* fell onto their knees and prayed. And why not; the sudden appearance of an unusual light in the night sky above them was reason enough to assume something supernormal was going on.

The phenomenon, whatever it was, must have been of limited duration, for Luke reports that the "angels" departed from them into heaven. That is, the light went away, and the shepherds decided to go down to Bethlehem to see what happened. They had observed a "big star" overhead and it had disappeared again, apparently rather soon after and quickly. What *did* the shepherds see?

Fortunately, we have a clue in the use of the Greek word *stratia,* rather than *astera. Stratia* means a light, small star, meteor, or a ball of fire, whereas *astera* would have been the word used, had a large star, planet, or other heavenly body of some importance appeared overhead.

Such a larger body would not appear suddenly, but would have been observed gradually, certainly over a matter of days and in other areas as well. Yet, this light only appeared in the immediate vicinity of Bethlehem!

The quick disappearance of the light also precludes any larger body. On the other hand, bolides and meteors, that is, hunks of metal and stone that fall from the sky and usually explode inside the atmosphere, fit the described phenomena better than any other natural occurrence.

Had they seen such a burst of light over their heads, marking the nearby town of Bethlehem, they would naturally have wondered what was going on down there. To them an exploding meteor was, of course, a "sign"—in the East natural phenomena always have mystic significance.

Meteors are usually too small or burn up too high in the atmosphere to cause great commotions among people, if they manage to fall in an inhabited area at all. Once in a while, of course, this cosmic dust does get down pretty far and causes excitement. The interpretation of such an event no longer requires Divine origin for it, but people, even in this twentieth century after His Advent, are frightened by unexplained events, and ever since man learned to make the instrument to destroy himself, man also fears that one of his kind might have just done so.

There are many and varied accounts of falling meteors and the people's reactions to them, ranging from medieval terror to modern curiosity. Typical perhaps was a large bolide exploding over the American coast on May 4, 1945. *The New York Post* reported the incident on that day without the slightest show of panic or concern, yet the undertone of nature's awesomeness cannot be overlooked:

"A mysterious blazing light in the skies, visible up and down the Eastern Seaboard and as far inland as Chicago, early today alerted civil and military authorities. But since no munition explosions were reported, it was generally believed to have been caused by a huge meteor. Although Philadelphia residents reported that their homes were rocked by the flash, the

Fordham University seismograph [according to Father J. Joseph Lynch] recorded two earth vibrations. Whatever it was must have taken place in the air, Father Lynch said.

"The blazing spectacle, which lasted only a second or two, most probably was caused by a bolide meteor, an official of Hayden Planetarium said. Such a meteor suddenly appears as a fireball, before exploding into millions of pieces. Often the fragments are never found, or crash into the ocean.

"From Annapolis, 'a blue ribbon of light about twenty feet wide with drifting fragments' was seen at 3:40 A.M. by Captain H. E. Avery, who was aboard his cabin cruiser in the harbor, the Associated Press reported. He said that a 'whoosh' accompanied the light, which disappeared into Chesapeake Bay toward the north. Dr. Olivier, head of the American Meteorological Society, said that he heard 'some explosion,' but did not know what it was. He said that such meteors commonly explode 18 to 20 miles in the air."

Other "falling stars," as they are poetically, but wrongly called at times, have been observed for several seconds before disintegrating. Only rarely do they last long enough in solid form to hit the earth, but there is this huge crater in Siberia and another one in Arizona to prove that it can happen. Luckily for the shepherds and townspeople of Bethlehem—and Him—this meteor, if it was a meteor, was of a smaller and less solid variety!

Most people think of "the Star of Bethlehem" as a "star" that appeared to both the shepherds *and* the three Kings. Yet the shepherds saw their "star" the day Christ was born, and the Kings, according to tradition, arrived twelve days later. No meteor lasts that long, and for that matter, neither does a conjunction or other heavenly fireworks. Even a comet might change position considerably in such a time.

I had an idea that there were indeed *two* "stars," not one, and decided to consult the acting director of New York's Hayden Planetarium, Miss Marian Lockwood. Readily, she pointed out that Kepler, sixteenth-century Polish astronomer, had also thought the Star to have been a meteor, at least at first. What changed the great astronomer's mind?

Johannes Kepler had just perfected a telescope and was scanning the heavens with it. The year was 1603. He became fascinated with the conjunction of Saturn and Jupiter in the sign Pisces. To the naked eye, it appeared as one large star, but in his telescope he could clearly distinguish the two planets approaching each other. Now planets move rather rapidly as different from "stars" (really suns), and a few days make a good deal of difference in the way a conjunction might appear from a terrestrial vantage point, especially with a telescope.

It occurred to Kepler that this same conjunction had also taken place when Christ was born. Could this have been "the Star of Bethlehem"? Consulting his charts, the astronomer found that the conjunction of Saturn and Jupiter in Pisces occurred in 7 B.C., three times, in fact, on May 29, October 3, and December 4.

Many people realize that Christ was not born in the year zero. The current Christian Era actually started six years before. The error came about through faulty calculations by the sixth-century historian Exiguus, one of those responsible for our calendar.

Pisces, the last and highest of the zodiac signs, was always considered by the ancients to be symbolic of destiny, religion, and mediumship. The conjunction of the two planets occurring in the sign of the fish would therefore be a natural moment for a religious leader to be born.

"Of course, there are other opinions about the Star," Miss Lockwood explained. "The astronomer Wieser thinks it was a *nova,* a suddenly forming star or sun, as we call it."

Novae are distant implosions of huge stars forming, which take millions of years to reach us. I doubt that such a light would have had the closeness and personal awe associated with it which by Luke's account the shepherds experienced.

The Star, Miss Lockwood thought, might have been a comet, one of those strange "wandering stars" which enter and leave our solar system irregularly.

The *Chinese Tables,* a usually accurate document of great antiquity, refer to a "nova" for about 6 B.C.

Nova or comet—these observations must refer to the Star the three Kings saw and not to the light encountered by the shepherds. If we assume that the two heavenly events were separate and not connected, everything takes on a different appearance and apparent contradictions can be resolved.

It is most likely that the first and original Christmas Eve did not occur on December 24, but at some other time of year.

Marguerite Steedman, in *Refuge in Avalon,* feels it

must have been October 3, 7 B.C., because the three Kings, arriving in the Holy Land some time after, would have been unable to travel in May, owing to the excessive heat in that part of the world. Also, the shepherds would not have been sleeping outdoors in the hills on the later date, December, when Palestine can have pretty chilly nights. Thus, October seems the most likely period.

There is also a tradition among mystics that the Christ would be born in the sign of the Balance, Libra. The physical descriptions of Jesus that have come down to us show him to have been youthful, slender, almost effeminate and extremely sensitive and emotional —all of which fits the Libra concept of birth. But even without recourse to astrological ideas and ideals it seems likely that the event occurred toward the end of the year 7 B.C., since other historical events, keyed in to fit this assumption, have checked out correctly.

News traveled reasonably fast even in those far-off Biblical days. An extraordinary event such as that experienced by the simple shepherds would eventually have become known to the authorities, especially Herod the king, who was not apt to overlook anything with the slightest tinge of the supernormal. Angel or meteor, it affected his position. But before this news reached Herod in Jerusalem, another event took place, *according to tradition,* exactly twelve days after the shepherds had seen the "light."

5

The Journey of The Magi

Now when Jesus was born in Bethlehem of Judaea in the days of Herod the king, behold, there came wise men from the east to Jerusalem, saying, Where is he that is born King of the Jews?"

Thus Matthew reports the appearance of strangers asking strange questions, for everybody in Jerusalem knew that it was not healthy to ask about a king other than Herod, and Herod had not become a father recently, nor would such a child be a King at birth.

This passage is the only contemporary news we have

of the Wise Men, or as they are sometimes styled, Wisemen, and it must be noted that the number of men is not mentioned. Nevertheless, in art and literature, they are always referred to as three, and they are named Caspar, Melchior, and Balthasar. They are sometimes called The Three Holy Kings and sometimes The Three Wisemen, being both royal and wise.

From the sixth-century mosaics to the 1951 opera *Amahl and the Night Visitors* by Gian-Carlo Menotti, the world has known of the gift-bearing Wisemen. Only during the past two centuries have we had really reliable and fast means of communication about events transpiring at a distance in both time and space. Thus we must rely on word of mouth or later retelling for the details of specific events that occurred almost two thousand years ago.

In the case of the Wisemen tradition, we have preciously little to go on, but what we have is clearly stated and there is actually no confusion or contradiction between various versions. The story is always told the same, whether by Western or Eastern people.

Strangely enough, the tradition of the Epiphany is not so strong in the country of its origin as it is elsewhere. This may be due to the confusing amalgamation of the celebration of the once-pagan solstice with the birthday of Jesus. In Palestine, there is no such pre-Christian tradition, since the Celtic-Germanic solstice did not have a counterpart among the Semitic people then inhabiting the Holy Land.

In Austria, children dress up as the Holy Kings, sing carols, and collect their somewhat enforced rewards at the door in the form of fruit and cake plat-

Caspar

ters. Instead of bringing gifts as did their ancient counterparts, the Central European children receive them. It is interesting to note that one of the three must always wear black face, as in paintings of the arrival of the Kings. All of these have a dark king among them, a tradition of such early origin that it appears to have been already well established in the period of the Ravenna mosaics, in the sixth century.

In the villages of Central Europe, it is still customary to chalk the letters K+M+B on the door, but one must make sure one does this very early in the morning, or Caspar, Melchior, and Balthasar will pass you by and fail to bless your house. Tradition has it that the Holy Kings rode during the day.

Matthew speaks of *magoi* or wisemen, not of kings. Marguerite Steedman and others assume the three men were astrologers from Mesopotamia, a view which completely ignores the tradition of "three *Kings*," one of them black. Astrologers served at the Courts of ancient kings, most of whom relied on astrology for their self-preservation. It is most unlikely, however, that there were three astrologers who rose to the throne to be the three Kings!

Somewhere between Matthew and the medieval art schools, the *magoi* or Wisemen turned into royalty. It must be borne in mind, however, that Matthew, unaccustomed to strangely dressed visitors possessed of superior knowledge, might have thought of them as wisemen first.

In any event, it was much safer in those days to be a simple traveler, even an astrologer, than to admit to being a king, for ransom jails awaited the unwary king traveling without protection. Were the trio royal, they certainly would not have broadcast their true status, especially as the reputation of their prospective host was a most unsavory one.

Matthew's account lends itself to ambiguity, unfortunately.

In the King James Version of the Bible, the passage is given as "When Jesus was born," but the Greek text may also be read, "Jesus having been born. . . ," thus establishing that the arrival of the three men was later than the birth. This construction could signify *anything from a few days to a couple of years.*

Matthew continues his account with another phrase I feel has been misunderstood: "We have seen his star in the east, and are come to worship him."

The question is, did they see "his star," whatever it was, while they themselves were in the East, or did they see the Star appear to the east of themselves?

The Greek original could also be translated as "We have seen his star *rising.*" One must remember that to an astrologer the rising sign, or ascendant, is of great importance for the future character of the one born under such a sign. Now, if they had seen "his star" rising, or in the east, coming themselves from that general direction, the question is what sort of star could they follow, what *sort* of *star in the east* would lead them to the Holy Land?

Certainly no ordinary star or planet would be outstanding enough to lure three astrologer kings from their presumably faraway lands.

Again, one must examine the evidence of tradition, since we have no direct pipeline to the past except for

Matthew. The paintings of the Journey of the Magi and of the Adoration of the Magi almost always show a star with a long golden tail, a comet. A very few show a bright star and two tiny stars farther back, a constellation, conjunction, or perhaps only a primitive attempt to represent a comet's tail. Not one painting shows a *single* bright star with the three Kings!

Some paintings of the shepherds also show the cometlike star with tail, but this may be due to the later amalgamation of the two events. As I have shown before, the two events could not possibly have been concerned with one and the same "star."

I had now become convinced that the Journey of the Kings took a long time and that they had indeed come from afar. If they had seen "his star" overhead all that time, it could not have been a conjunction. Only a comet would stay in the sky for a period of weeks or months. The *Chinese Tables* report a comet in 4 B.C. This may be a different comet, or perhaps it reappeared. It may also be that the "nova" reported by the same source for 6 B.C., and this comet, were one and the same event. We cannot be entirely sure of the *Chinese Tables* in this respect, but a conjunction of Jupiter and Saturn, however attractive such a solution would have been astrologically, may not be the answer.

The visitors threw Herod into a state of shock. He had never heard either of a star behaving so strangely, or indeed of the imminent birth of another king of the Jews. Understandably, he was worried. Summoning his advisers, including of course astrologers, he berated them for not having told him about these events. Evidently word of the Bethlehem "light" had not gotten through to them as yet, or was not considered important. But they cited an old prophecy, according to which Bethlehem would someday be the place where a ruler over Judaea would see the light of day. This was not very encouraging, in fact it was extremely vague, so Herod decided to query his foreign visitors. Perhaps they knew more than his own people.

Matthew puts it this way in the King James Version:

"Then Herod, when he had privily called the wisemen, inquired of them diligently what time the star appeared."

What Herod was reported to have asked, according to the Greek text, was "at what time" did the star (first) appear. By that he meant not what time of day, but what season, even what year.

We have no record of their reply, but surely it must have been a matter of months since the three visitors had first glimpsed the star in their own country or countries. Evidently their reply satisfied the suspicious monarch, for he asked them to go to Bethlehem and look for the child they had come to worship, then report back to him so he could join them in this pious pursuit.

Their original query for the "King of the Jews" must be understood in Eastern terms. Anyone having been born under such auspices would automatically be of royal origin. In a civilization where the ruler was also a demi-god, or at least a high priest, such thinking was natural. The trio did not come directly to Herod's palace in Jerusalem. They entered the city, Matthew

Citadel, Jerusalem

tells us, and made inquiries for him "that is born King of the Jews." Their inquiries were reported to Herod and he summoned them to the palace. Later, as we have observed, Jesus referred to himself as "King of the Jews," meaning it surely in the spiritual sense, and his tormentors also put the letters INRI over the cross, meaning in Latin, Jesus the Nazarene, King of the Jews.

I was faced with a most curious proposition. Although I had not yet found proof of the origin of the three men, I was somehow deeply convinced that they existed, moreover, that they came from different places and that these places were not particularly close to the Holy Land.

This Star of the Wisemen puzzled me. They had seen it, in the east or from the east, yet the people of the western country, that is the Holy Land, had not. What sort of heavenly body can be seen only from a distance and not from the area over which it seems to travel?

According to astronomers, a phenomenon of this sort is seen by all people living on the same latitude. For instance, India, Ethiopia, and Southern Arabia, which are all on approximately the same latitude though widely separated geographically, might observe the comet from their 20-degree "line"—but Palestine, the Holy Land, being on a different latitude, would not see it.

However, the Holy Land is not too far from what astronomers call "the line of best visibility" and thus might see the comet also under good conditions, while people in the best visibility areas would see it far more prominently. In Palestine, it might only appear as a star among stars and not create any stir at all. It was not until the strangers called attention to the "star," the comet, that Herod and his people became aware of it. Even then they had trouble locating it and asked the help of the three Wisemen to find the "star" that had brought them to Palestine. The visitors obviously knew what it looked like and presumably would be able to point it out to Herod among many similar-looking heavenly bodies.

When the audience with Herod had ended, later during that morning, the three visitors decided to continue on their way without delay. For they did not trust Herod, and besides they were eager to see the child.

Now, Bethlehem is only a short distrance from Jerusalem, but in those days the roads were not the best and travel on horseback would have taken them a few hours to reach their destination. Apparently they lost sight of the comet at this point. Barely visible in Palestinian skies, it was even less visible in the daytime. But Herod had told them about the Bethlehem prophecy, so they had to look there first.

Although Matthew does not talk about their difficulties in finding the "star" again, local tradition does. According to Madeleine S. and J. Lane Miller's *Encyclopedia of Bible Life,* the Kings did not get their bearings again until they reached the so-called *Well of the Magi* on the outskirts of Bethlehem. It had grown dark in the meantime, and they saw the reflection of "their" star in the water of the well near which they rested. Encouraged by this sign, they continued their quest and shortly after arrived in Bethlehem.

Well of the Magi

Matthew reports the incident somewhat differently:

"Lo, the star, which they saw in the east, went before them, till it came and stood over where the young child was."

The tradition, we have seen, has the Holy Kings pass "through" during the day, not during the morning. That is why Europeans especially mark their doors K+M+B in the morning, to make sure the passing Kings won't miss them.

With Bethlehem lying to the southwest of Jerusalem and the comet seemingly moving "before them," that is from east to west, roughly speaking, Matthew's account would be accurate. His report that the "star . . . came and stood over where the young child was" does pose some difficulty. Comets do not stop in mid-air even on so solemn an occasion.

The original Greek wording is *"elthon esté"* which Dr. Berry translates as "having come and fixed." The word *esté,* derived from the verb *histemi,* means "stood" only in its secondary sense. Primarily it means to mark, to fix. Thus, the comet appeared and passed over the inn, thereby fixing the spot where the child was. Just remember how often the moon seems to pass just over your rooftop, yet it is quite far away.

The proper wording then should be "the comet passed over and marked the spot where the young child was"!

With the help of this natural phenomenon the three visitors finally found the manger and presented their gifts to the child. Matthew reports that they had been "Divinely instructed in a dream" that they should not return to Herod and tell him about the child. Perhaps they had indeed been warned in what is known in psychic terms as a premonitory dream. There is nothing supernatural in having sixth-sense experiences transcending the ordinary boundaries of time and space. But even if the three visitors did not have such a psychic message, their common sense must have told them not to go back to the tyrant and endanger the life of the child. Instead, according to the King James Version of Matthew, "they departed into their own country by another way."

This has usually been taken to mean they departed into one and the same country, the three of them, but the Bible does not say so at all. The Greek wording, *"eis tehn choran auton,"* means literally "into the country of themselves," or in plain English, into their respective countries.

"Di' allehs hodou" literally means "by a different way," but taken together with the first part of the passage, it can also mean "by different ways." In other words, they split up—not only because they had different countries to go to, as will be seen later, but perhaps also to make it more difficult for any pursuer.

During the time of Christ, the term "magi," or *magoi* in Greek, which is roughly equivalent to our term for magician, often referred to Persian astrologers. Thus we have the concept of the three Kings being astrologers from the East. Marguerite Steedman cites as proof of this identification the excavations of clay tablets recording the Saturn-Jupiter conjunction of 7 B.C.

These tablets were unearthed at an ancient school for astrologers, at Sippar, Babylonia. Great importance had been attached to this conjunction, it is true, but from the astrologer's point of view, all life and all events in people's and even countries' lives are determined, guided, and explained by the position of the planets, and the sun and moon. It is entirely possible that the conjunction set the stage for the birth of the Messiah, but I am inclined to accept the comet, in addition, as the visible "star" the three Kings followed.

That they were not Persian astrologers, but men of royal blood, I was sure of—but how could I prove it?

6
Who Were the Three Kings?

WHENEVER I stopped a conversation at a party or among my friends with the remark that I thought there *really were* three Wisemen, I was looked at with varying degrees of doubt.

The work done by archaeologists in recent years in the Holy Land has helped make things a little easier for us. After all, the Dead Sea Scrolls, the rediscovery of King Solomon's mines, his relationship with the Queen of Sheba, and many more incidents reported in the Bible that turned out to be authentic, have lately made us look at The Book with somewhat different eyes.

The Bible is not a supernormal instrument directly created by God. It is a collection of writings by mortal men who were the inspired messengers of truth, and is a tangible historical document and must be taken as such. It is our duty to sift the true from the false, or merely hearsay material or later distortions from the original texts, and in general prove that some, although not all, of the events in the Bible are historically authentic.

The Wisemen existed as men of flesh and blood, and it was my desire to find convincing proof that they were more than a legend, that they had indeed once walked on earth as men. But where was I to begin?

The first modern work referring to the Wisemen was an obscure publication of the *Rhenan Museum for Philology* series in which Professor A. von Gutschmidt, the archaeologist, discussed "the royal names in the apocryphic apostle legends." This 1864 publication, in German, contains an evaluation of the so-called "Lists of Wise Men from the East" given in Hyde's *History of the Religions of Ancient Persia*. There are lots of "wisemen" in this list, but Gutschmidt correctly recognized them as nothing more than the names of governors of the thirteeen Persian provinces during the time of Jesus. The Persian governors, or satraps, wore peculiar headgear similar to the highpriests of the Jews, and perhaps this gave rise to the notions that Persian officials were wisemen or magi.

The number of Wisemen as three, and their names, must have fairly early origins, since Byzantine mosaics were already depicting and naming them.

But how early?

Bible scholar J. Lane Miller, whom I met several years before his untimely death, had the answer for me:

"A depiction of the wisemen was centuries ago placed in the mosaic façade of the Church of the Nativity at Bethlehem. When the Persians attacked Bethlehem in 614 A.D., they are said to have spared the Church of the Nativity because they saw in its mosaic façade the likeness of their own turbaned selves."

It is interesting to note that the mosaics in the Church of Sant' Appolinare in Classe at Ravenna, Italy, which was built about 500 A.D., are similar to the ones at Bethlehem. They also show three turbaned Wisemen led by a star, approaching the enthroned Madonna with Child with their gifts. Their names appear above the scene. The Ravenna mosaics are generally assigned to the period of the rule of Justinian, 527-565 A.D.

On all representations of this scene, the three men walk or appear in the same order. Caspar or Gaspard is first, Melchior second, and Balthasar brings up the rear. Gaspard is always tall, old, and nearly always shown bearded. Melchior is always a young man without a beard. Balthasar is always black-skinned or very dark, and small in stature. Only in Sassetta's painting, "Journey of the Magi," does he appear as a white man, but dressed in black attire.

What were the origins of the names traditionally attached to the three Wisemen? In the English language the names are Caspar or Gaspard, Melchior, and Balthasar, but in other tongues Gaspard is better known as Kaspar, Kasper, or Gasparro, and even Gepard.

I consulted another source, rarely used: A. von Sallet's article on the successors of Alexander the Great in Bactria and India, published in Berlin in 1880. He translated Melchior as "king of light," Balthasar as "the chaldaic name for Daniel," and he had no explanation for Gaspard. But it sounded "Indo-Parthian" to him as it did to Gutschmidt.

I took a hard look at these names and tried to analyze them linguistically. Gaspard or Caspar sounded Persian, which in the period here under discussion was "Indo-Parthian," the language used in an area including what is now eastern Iran, Afghanistan, and western India.

Melchior sounded Semitic. I compared it with Melk or Melik, which means either great or king. The name Balthasar was more difficult to understand.

Bal was a Phoenician deity, but I could not find a Phoenician name similar to Balthasar. It occurred to me that perhaps the Syrian Christians, who succeeded the Phoenicians, might have assimilated a strange name to the nearest they could find locally. The story of the Wisemen was first spread by Syrian Christians and we must respect their renditions of names as being first-hand.

Soon I discovered other clues. It was like a jig-saw puzzle, and slowly it started to fall into place.

It was a cold winter night just before Christmas, two days before the feast, in fact, when my thoughts were somehow drawn toward a traditional image of the three Wisemen I had placed into the folder marked

"Wisemen." I realized that Gaspard or Caspar was always shown as old, bearded, and rather venerable, truly the most characteristic of the *wise* men. Wisdom to the ancients was almost synonymous with East. Even the early Christians considered the East the direction whence knowledge came. Had not Jesus fulfilled the old prophecy, *"ex oriente lux,"* "out of the east comes light," by proclaiming himself *"ego sum lux mundi,"* "I am the Light of the World"? In the literal sense, the sun was meant, for it rose in the east and shed light upon the west, but on the deeper, esoteric level, the ancients always expected their Messiah from an *easterly* direction.

An Arab or Phoenician was a close neighbor to the Palestinian Jew. A king from such an area would hardly be referred to as coming "from the east." Caspar must have been from a country much farther removed. If the name was Indo-Parthian, then our first Wiseman came from what is now roughly Afghanistan, far indeed from Judaea.

Melchior, the middle Wiseman, was certainly Semitic, but there were many Maliks and Melks ranging from what is now Turkey to the southern tip of Arabia and into North Africa as well. The quoted traditional connotations of Melchior as "king of light" interested me. In the Zoroastrian religion, then already on the rise, the world consists of Ereb or Europe and Asia, which means Light. By Asia, the first century understood what we now call the Near East. Thus, "the king of light" would be a ruler of the Near East.

As for Balthasar, the last of the trio, his dark skin, small stature, a usually flat nose, and Negroid

Jerusalem

features made it obvious that he was an African. In the first century, Greek culture and a white Greek upper class largely dominated the countries of the Mediterranean. History records very few native black princes as having had any relationship with the Greek world around them. With all of North Africa dominated by the white man—either Greek, Phoenician, Berber, or Roman—one would have to look for a really powerful black ruler much farther south.

There may have been tribal princes galore, but the only king of any stature known in the ancient world who was certainly black was the Emperor of Ethiopia. The Amhari, who are basically white people, had not yet conquered the area now known as Ethiopia or Abyssinia, and a darker race dominated the country's destiny. They were a powerful race of warriors who had also managed to bring parts of Southern Arabia under their control.

Was the third Wiseman then the Emperor, or Negus Negesti, of Ethiopia?

7

The Gifts of The Magi

I NOW wanted to examine the gifts the three Kings had brought the Christ child. Obviously in analyzing the products, clues as to their origin might be obtained.

Caspar brought *gold*. Matthew reports this, and the ancients generally considered the fabulous and mysterious land Ophir the place where there was lots of the yellow metal. In the days of King Solomon, the Queen of Sheba, later one of his wives, sent her ships from Southern Arabia to Ophir to fetch gold.

Some historians have identified Ophir as East Africa, but there are many reasons against it. In the first place, why should the Queen of Sheba send ships across the Red Sea when she could just as easily obtain gold from overland? After all, the South Arabian territory of Ethiopia was her neighbor. Then, too, East Africa never had any reputation for large gold deposits. To this day most African gold comes from faraway South Africa. But India did have then and still has many gold mines and to send ships to India would have been the only practical way for the Queen to get her gold. Then, too, the word Ophir has Indo-Parthian connotations. I was convinced that Caspar came from the general direction of India.

Frankincense was Melchior's gift to the babe. The lexicon defines this substance as "the pith of the frankincense tree, boswellia, which, when heated, gives out a characteristic odor." In ancient times this aromatic was found mainly in the "frankincense country" called Punt. Where was Punt?

Again I turned to Dr. Miller's *Encyclopedia of Bible Life*: "The great spice caravans brought frankincense from various parts of the world to Palestine and one of the few great trading centers, where the caravans from India and Southern Arabia used to meet and stop over, is *Petra,* capital of the Nabataean Arabs."

Were Petra and Punt one and the same?

I looked at the map. Certainly any trader coming from Southern Arabia or India would have to go via Petra in order to reach Jerusalem. The route via Syria was far more hazardous and lacked the trading

Petra Desert

possibilities en route which the way along the desert offered. I recalled the traditional pictures of the Wisemen *traveling in the desert,* with the "star" leading them onward. Were they based on truth?

Balthasar, the black king, offered the Christ child *myrrh.* This aromatic is "the pith of African-Arabian bushes and trees, used as incense, and growing on both sides of the Red Sea." *Both sides of the Red Sea!* Something in my mind clicked. A black king who ruled both sides of the Red Sea and an aromatic coming from that area. It fit together well.

I was pretty sure now that the nationality of the Wisemen could be identified as Indian, Arabic, and Ethiopian.

Other elements needed to be clarified. Why, for example, were they called "magi"? Could it be that the Phrygian caps—the forerunner of the eighteenth-century Liberty Cap—worn by the Kings created the impression that they were of Persian origin? In Palestine, such a cap symbolized priesthood or mysticism, hence the term *magi* or astrologers. But in India the same cap was worn as part of the royal crown, as shown by the coins of the period. Incidentally, only on the Ravenna mosaics do all three wear the cap; elsewhere it is the tall Caspar, with the other two wearing different symbols of royalty.

And what of the comet? How long could one comet remain visible? A conjunction would not be in the sky for sufficiently long times to allow the three Wisemen to observe it and use it as a guiding star. At the Hayden Planetarium I learned that the comet of 4 B.C. reported by the *Chinese Tables* lasted seventy days.

If this was the right comet—or perhaps the one also reported as a "nova" in 6 B.C.—and it could be observed in China for seventy days, then it may well have been still visible in Palestine by the time the trio reached there. Traditionally, the trip took seven months from India—from Caspar's country—to Jerusalem. Certainly, several months had elapsed between the time the first of the trio started and their joint arrival in Bethlehem.

But did they really arrive only twelve days after the shepherds had hailed the birth of Jesus?

I am inclined to think that a far longer period of time elapsed between the two events. Had not Herod given orders later to kill all male children in Bethlehem, two years and under? If the Christ child had been only twelve days old by the time the Wisemen arrived to worship him, there would have been no need for such a sweeping order. On the other hand, if several months had gone by, Herod might have played it safe and had a wider age bracket included in his murderous order. For the sake of a better story—both verbally and pictorially—tradition puts the arrival of the Wisemen closer to the adoration of the shepherds. The Bible wording, which does not mention the time lag between the two events, is such that months, even a couple of years, could have passed before the trio made their appearance. Were the *Chinese Tables* right, after all, did the "nova" of 6 B.C. concern the "star" of the shepherds, and the comet of 4 B.C. the comet of the Wisemen?

Nothing in Matthew indicates that the Wisemen found the Christ child in the manger. Hardly—especially if up to two years had gone by since the birth!

Jerusalem

Whether Herod was misinformed in assuming that as much time as two years had gone by since the birth or whether it actually was that much later when the three Wisemen arrived in Palestine, the fact remains that Herod *did* order all two-year-olds and under murdered. The Flight into Egypt may therefore very well have taken place quite a bit later than is generally assumed. Certainly the artistic concept of the three Kings visiting the babe *in the manger* seems fictional to me.

Why was it that neither Luke nor Matthew reported *both* events, the adoration of the shepherds and the arrival of the three Kings? Luke wrote only of the shepherds and Matthew only of the Kings. The two Evangelists were not far apart in time, so the events must have been equally fresh in both their minds. It is of course possible that the events were identical and were only seen in different ways by two different men.

Since there were other events that were not duplicated in the four gospel accounts, it occurred to me that some skillful hand might have edited them to avoid duplication. After all, we do know that the versions of the four Gospels we now use were developed over a long period and are the work not of a single inspired source, but of a number of anonymous scribes with varying skills, viewpoints, and educational backgrounds.

None of the authors of the four Gospels knew Jesus as a small child, of course, so there were no eyewitnesses of the adoration of either shepherds or Magi among them. They concentrated their accounts on the adult life of Jesus, with which they might have been personally familiar, sketching only fleeting descriptions of the birth and childhood of their leader.

The Gospels were composed several decades after the death of Jesus, probably even later, and by that time the event itself must have been colored by distortions. Unfortunately, the parents of the Christ child did not write their own version of the miraculous events attending the birth of their offspring.

Matthew, the tax collector, must have had access to information on the Holy Family for purposes of census and taxation, and this was the aspect of the event that interested *him* most. Luke, on the other hand, as physician and scientist, was fascinated by the Star and the experiences of the shepherds.

If both events—the Star of the shepherds and the Star of three Wisemen—had occurred about the same time, surely they would have been recorded by Matthew *and* Luke. But if the two occurrences were two years apart, Luke might have felt that the adoration of the Magi was not properly concerned with the birth of Jesus itself and left it out in his account of *that* event.

On the other hand, Matthew, the government official, attached far more importance to the arrival of foreign dignitaries than to the excitement of a handful of ignorant shepherds. He would naturally record the arrival of the three Kings, but might not care to mention the shepherds.

8

What's in the Stars?

It is one thing for a group of semiliterate, superstitious shepherds to be aroused by a "big light" and to come down from their mountains a few miles to see what happened in the town below, but for three important personalities to travel several months merely because of a "star" is an entirely different matter. Only by realizing the great impact that astrology, which included astronomy, had on the lives of the people of the first century can we find a clue to their motivation.

In a world in which astrology was part of everyday life, nobody had to guess about the meaning of heavenly fireworks. If something unusual appeared in the sky, the competent astrologers of every country made their interpretations known and that was that. Astrology as the ancients practiced it was the forerunner of modern astronomy as well.

The stars have always played a major role in the destinies of men, whether people accept astrology as factual or merely a fanciful plaything that amuses without proof.

Julius Caesar ignored the warning to take care of himself on the Ides of March and paid for it with his life. Dozens of astrologers knew that President Kennedy was in personal danger around the time of his assassination, yet nothing could be done to prevent it. It looks almost as if Fate does not allow interference with its course set in motion by forces greater than the individuals themselves.

The planets are composed of varying matter, mainly metals and minerals, some of which are what we call radioactive while others may be only mildly so. No two planets are alike in composition. Is it therefore so farfetched to think that radiation from these comparatively close-by bodies can influence life on this planet earth? We all know how one atomic bomb exploded over Hiroshima has tragically altered the lives of innocent generations, not to mention those who were present when it happened. Likewise, cosmic radiation does influence personal characteristics, both physical and emotional. This is not a matter of speculation, but a proven scientific fact.

The relative position of these planets toward each other, and toward man on earth at any given moment, will change continuously. Consequently, the nature of this radiation will also change in both intensity and direction, creating different effects all the time. This, I feel, is behind the reality of astrology, the influence of cosmic radiation exerted on a child at the very moment when it takes its first breath outside the protection of the mother's womb.

The stars impel, but do not compel—that is, we are subject to their influences but retain our power of reaction to these influences as we see fit, as we are able to, depending on our mental, emotional, and physical abilities. This is true, I think, although destinies are outlined in broad strokes ahead of us, ahead of the time when we actually experience these conditions. Our reaction to them will determine our future. It is a moot question whether even this reaction of ours is predestined by a superhuman force beyond our ken, or whether we do have this limited power of decision, of free will. Perhaps the individual does not count as much in the larger scheme of things as does the "action" itself.

If everybody's "number" were determined before his time and death occurs when it is meant to happen, then no other view would explain why apparently unrelated individuals die together in airplane tragedies or other large holocausts. Did the Finger of Fate pick a number of "types" that were to be eliminated at that time and an airplane accident was as good a method as any to do it "economically"?

Or was each and every person earmarked for the

transition called death carefully guided to take his seat on the fateful plane and were those not meant to be along for the ride just as carefully prevented from taking it?

Whether or not God personally supervises this "operation," His Law certainly guides our lives. The planets, and in outer space, the stars, also are part of Divine Creation. Consequently, could not the guidelines supplied by the movements of the planets, and interpreted by competent astrologers, be God's way of helping man a little to understand his destiny? A small glimpse, perhaps, into eternity, to bring out the best in us?

Ancient astrologers were superb mathematicians who never made any rash predictions. A person of standing, especially of royal blood, had access to the very best astrological information. What the official astrologers told the people about the mystic significance of heavenly events differed from that which they reported privately to their rulers.

There might be a deeper meaning to the movements of the planets, sun, moon, and distant stars, but the educated person knew full well that no Phoebus Apollo was riding in a golden chariot across the sky, and Mars really wasn't a bearded warrior, but a copper-rich planet.

It is less than four hundred years since Galileo Galilei asserted his conviction that the earth moved around the sun, and not vice versa, yet the truly educated ancients had no doubts about this fact. It did not, however, change their astrological zodiac, which, after all, was nothing more than a mathematical convenience, just as time is a convenient device to allow us to regulate our lives.

Thus, the three Magi might have been impressed by the appearance of a comet, and they might have felt that it signified some important event in history. But was the appearance of this itinerant heavenly body enough of a reason to risk their precious lives in a difficult journey from far away, just to check up on something as vague as an "important birth"?

The Oriental is by nature a trader. The three Kings brought the Christ child samples of their products. Obviously, they must have had more than the samples with them. The Bible does not shed light on this nor does it mention any servants or companions coming to Jerusalem. But it was not unusual in this period for an important trader to "anchor" his ships of the desert, his camels, or sometimes his horses, outside the city, where he could quickly alert his people if danger were imminent. Once within the city walls, this might be impossible. If the three Kings had any caravan with them, they would certainly have left them well outside Herod's greedy grasp. *I felt sure the three men had not come for the comet's sake alone.*

"Caravans of spice and myrrh in Old Testament times went from the Persian Gulf across Arabia to Petra, in its mountain fastness south of the Dead Sea, and thence to Gaza," Dr. Miller observed.

This southern route would have been taken by anyone coming from India or Afghanistan. From the Persian Gulf across to the Arab Peninsula, they would continue to the desert city of Petra. An old tradition says that the three Kings met in the desert. My feeling is that they met at Petra, either by design or accident, or rather that Petra was the real starting point for the expedition to Jerusalem.

Today, Petra is a secondary tourist attraction within the territory of Jordan. The connoisseurs among the traveling public will go there to marvel at the stark reality of the cliffs and the bleached, white ruins of ancient cities embedded between the rocks. The average tourist satisfied with a look at the Eiffel Tower and the Coliseum will probably never get to Petra.

Two thousand years ago, the Nabataean capital was of course far more of a bustling city than it is today. To begin with, its strategic position at the edge of the desert, and yet not of the desert, gave it the enviable role of a sophisticated intermediary between the harshness of the immense Arabian Desert and the fleshpots of Egypt and Palestine.

A man could relax in Petra and the Nabataeans of the first century were people of the world.

These western Arabs also knew the advantages of canalization and they made the desert bloom the way the Israelis do today in their part of the world. In a way, then, the Nabataean Kingdom of the first century A.D. was a civilized way station where anyone coming in from the south would want to rest up before continuing onward. The western Arabs made shrewd use of this vantage point: their trade was brisk and voluminous and the well-built cities still dotting the country like bright beacons attest to their talents as city dwellers. The royal tombs compare favorably with those of neighboring Egypt. Even the dead were treated well in Petra.

Caspar had come from India, probably at the head

of a small caravan. Normally, such a trade mission would have been led by a responsible official, but the appearance of the comet might have aroused the King's curiosity to the point of leading the caravan himself.

The dark-skinned King, whom I believed to be the ruler of Ethiopia, also had a good enough reason to come to Petra.

Since the marriage of the Queen of Sheba to Solomon of Judaea, five hundred years earlier, their son Menelik and all his successors had ruled over Ethiopia as well as Sheba's Southern Arabia. This was not without occasional difficulties. We have reports of the Negus' appearance among his Arab subjects, on horseback, trying to impress them with his power. Trading was brisk between both coasts of the Red Sea. He, too, might have seen the comet or heard of its appearance, and decided to travel in the direction in which it had been observed. The first major stop on the Journey to Jerusalem would have been Petra.

I also felt that the middle King was an Arab. He was always represented as a young man and I wondered whether the Petraean Arabs had a king so young. Had the two foreign dignitaries arrived at Petra and been joined there by someone of royal blood, perhaps a prince? On some of the pictures of the arrival of the Magi, they are shown on camelback, and that would have been their mode of transportation had they come from Petra. Nobody traveled all the way from India by camel, so Caspar must have exchanged his speedy horse for the slow camel somewhere along the route. Why not in Petra?

9

St. Thomas and the Oldest Christian Coins

IF THE three Kings really were rulers, and not mere astrologers, they would have left some monuments with their names on them. Unfortunately, the excavations in the Kabul area have thus far not yielded anything clearly identifying Caspar as a king in that region.

But there *is* something else. On many occasions, bronze coins bearing the name and likeness of a king named *Gondophares* had been found in and around Kabul. Now it is axiomatic in numismatics that frequent finds of coins in a given area denote that the coins were used in that area. Gondophares must have been a king in ancient Kabul.

I wondered whether this Gondophares and the Biblical Caspar were not the same man. If I could prove that they were, we would have the first contemporary portraits of *the man who saw Christ as a baby!*

I was by no means the only person who felt there was a connection. Over a hundred years ago the English archaeologist Cunningham had written an article in the *Journal of the Asiatic Society of Bengal,* in which he pointed out that the Gondophares known only from coins must be the same king Gundaforus mentioned in the *Acta S. Thomas Apostoli,* or the Legend of St. Thomas, as it is called in English. This third-century document deals with the life of St. Thomas, whom the Indian Christians consider their patron saint.

Ten years later in 1865, the German scholar von Gutschmidt elaborated on Cunningham's findings and proved beyond doubt that the Gondophares of the coins and the Gundaforus mentioned in the Legend of St. Thomas were one and the same person.

Had anyone else written about the King? Indeed, in 1880, Professor von Sallet confirmed the earlier findings, as did the British scholar Whitehead in 1914.

Why the Greek-sounding name for a ruler of Afghan Kabul?

Under the powerful Parthian king Mithradates, the Persians then called Parthians had extended their rule deep into India and Afghanistan. They had managed to drive back the invading Scythians from the north.

Some Parthian princes or nobles for a long time managed to maintain their rule in Western India in opposition to the barbarous Scythians. Gradually, they had become independent of the Parthian kings, but still used Greek as their Court language even though their subjects spoke native dialects not related to European languages.

Perhaps the most important of these first-century rulers was Gondophares. He had managed to found a dynasty of his own; his nephew Abdagases appears with him on some of his coins, and another close relative and successor named Orthagnes has also been established through the numismatic route. Their coins are frequently found together, and in appearance, style, and workmanship belong to the same period and area.

Interestingly, the Legend of St. Thomas also speaks of Gundaforus' nephew *Labdanes* and a brother named *Gad*—different spellings of the names, for sure, but spellings differed a great deal in those days.

We do not have, thus far, any monument saying specifically that their good king Gondophares went to Jerusalem to follow a *Star in the East*. We do have an inscription in stone, however, unearthed at the site of Takht-i-Bahi, near Peshawar, on the border between what is now Pakistan and Afghanistan. This stone inscription gives Gondophares at least twenty-six years of reign, again fitting with the picture of an aged king for Caspar.

I asked myself, how does Gondophares become Caspar?

Even the ancients weren't sure how to spell his

name. We have records of Hyndopherres, Indophernes, Gundaphorus, and finally, Gadaspar. In the Middle Ages, the form Gaspard became popular. Professor R. B. Whitehead stated that in his view, the name Gondophares, in Greek, became Vindapharna in Persian. The ancient Armenians, using a totally different alphabet and system of sounds, styled it Gathaspar.

This was no isolated view. Leafing through other respected sources, I found that Justi, in his German-language *History of Iran*, fully agrees with this explanation. The great numismatic scholar, Percy Gardner, placed Caspar or Gondophares into the area around Kabul and Peshawar and from the style of the coins asserts that they must be of first-century origin. The royal family name Sasan does appear on them, and the designs are a mixture of Greek and Indian mythological representations.

But toward the very end of his rule, something must have happened that changed the appearance of the coins. For the first time, the king's portrait appears on his money, showing him as a bearded, aged, hollow-boned man.

Very little is known about the Legend of St. Thomas. Somebody may be referred to as a "doubting Thomas," but Thomas, far from staying a doubter, became one of the new religion's most ardent workers.

In the Thomas legend, we hear of a king of India named Gundaforus who finds himself in need of a good carpenter for a new palace he was building. He sends his nephew Labdanes (the Abdagases of the coin inscriptions) to Jerusalem.

It struck me at once that the king was going a

bit far afield for some carpentry, but Palestine was, of course, a center of learning and perhaps the king wanted something special designed. More likely, he wanted news of the child he had visited some years before. Had he heard that this child had grown into a young man named Jesus, by profession a carpenter? Was he hoping that Jesus himself would come to India?

We have no documents, of course, to prove that the king had direct written contact or even oral contact with Jesus. But the fact is that Thomas, one of Jesus' favorite disciples, was a fellow carpenter. Thomas did go to India and formally converted the king and his family to the new religion.

Not much is left of this early Christian community in the heart of today's Afghanistan. But my curiosity was aroused and coins were my tools. I was satisfied that the coins of Gondophares-Caspar showed the authentic portrait of the first of the three Kings. But what about the Christian community Thomas created? Should there not be some reference to this on the money of the period? After all, in an age before newspapers, books, radios, and television, the pictures and inscriptions on the money of the realm would be the main means of issuing propaganda and information about important events.

I went through the British Museum collections in search of a clue, but none of the money of the period offered anything out of the ordinary. One day my eyes fell upon a group of coins in my collection, coins which are unusually plentiful today as if they had been issued in quantities far beyond the needs of the period.

COINS OF CHRISTIAN SIGNIFICANCE

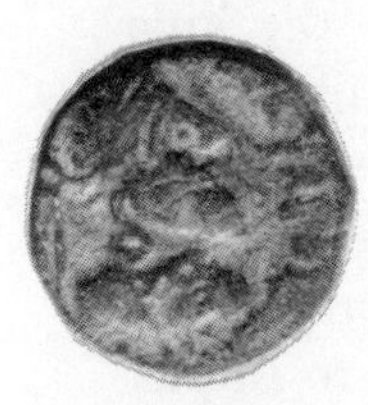

Bronze coin of King Gondophares (Caspar)

Bronze coin of Soter Megas, "The Great Saviour"

Bronze lepton (Widow's Mite) of Herod's time

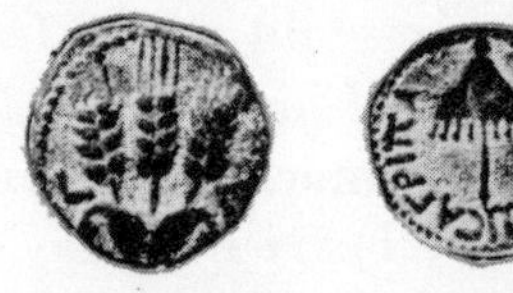

Bronze lepton current under Herod Agrippa, time of the Wisemen

Earliest "portrait" of Jesus on Byzantine bronze follis circa 1000 A.D.

These bronze coins are similar in appearance and style to the coins of Gondophares-Caspar and undoubtedly belong to the same period. But instead of the king's portrait, they show a portrait which runs the gamut from young to old and smooth to rough, and which is always surrounded by a circle of rays. I soon realized that this was no portrait at all but an artist's varying concept of a deity.

On the back of the coins we see a man on horseback, but on some of the better-made specimens, the horse becomes a camel.

It occurred to me that an inexperienced Indian diemaker, who had never seen a camel, would depict it in varying degrees of accuracy. But a camel it certainly is, or should be. This horseman type is similar to the traditional representation of the king on most Indian coins of that century, except for one detail. Other kings hold in their hand an ancus or scepter, but enlarged photographs clearly showed that *this* king held aloft a cross!

Now I was really eager to learn more about the coins. I discovered, for instance, that no other coins of India in antiquity show such a wide range of style and workmanship as do these strange coins with a king holding a cross. Nor is there any other precedent for a radiate deity appearing on the front of the coins. The inscription, in Greek, was strange, too. Surrounding the royal horseman, it reads, "Basileus Basileon Soter Megas," which, according to old-line numismatists, translates into, "King of Kings, Soter Megas." They simply assumed that Soter Megas was the *name* of a ruler, although nobody could trace such a king in either history or monuments.

In the 1930's, one Frank Higgins published a little pamphlet in which he claimed that the coins of this unknown king were really commemorative coins issued by the priests of India to commemorate the coming of Jesus.

The inscription, literally translated, reads, "King of Kings, our Great Savior"—and at once things fell into place for me.

No wonder nobody could trace this mysterious "Soter Megas"—there was no such name. A new deity had appeared in India, and to the traditional diemakers, some form of representation was necessary even though the early Judaeo-Christian religion frowned on portraits of the deity.

The spiritual, impersonal face surrounded by the rays of the sun was the diemaker's idea of what this new God might look like. The king riding a camel on the back of the coin, holding aloft the cross, referred to the new religion which by then had already become known in Asia. The cross, even if it was not yet the main symbol of Christianity, and an inscription praising the new deity, were in keeping with the practices of the time. This was India's way of letting the people, and the world, know that a Great Savior had come!

My conviction that these coins were indeed references to Jesus was strengthened shortly after when I deciphered a curious monogram appearing prominently on both sides of the coins.

Most coins of Bactria and India—Bactria is the Greek name for Eastern Persia and Western India—have some sort of royal monogram on them. But the Soter Megas were different. Turning the coin around by 90 degrees, the monogram spells out the Greek word "theos." *God.*

I looked at the man on the camel with a powerful magnifying glass. He wears a Phrygian cap, just as Caspar does in most of the paintings. I checked what the British Museum's Dr. Percy Gardner had thought about the period in which the "Great Savior" coins were issued. He had suggested that they were contemporary with the coins of Gondophares-Caspar and dated them after 30 A.D. This is the period shortly after Jesus' death, and it fits in well with the timetable of Caspar's journey.

I had some doubts about the cross as a Christian symbol at so early a period, but I discovered that the cross actually precedes the Christian Era as a symbol of suffering dating back to the Bronze Age. Were these coins issued to honor Caspar's formal conversion to Christianity? Were they connected with the visit of Thomas to India? Had not Jesus been called the "King of the Jews" in the spiritual sense? The commemorative coins, in effect, may be read "The Great Messiah is the King of Kings" rather than *our* king.

Was the aged Caspar yielding his royal prerogative of portraiture on his coins to the new deity? Had he brought the cross from afar and was this being shown on the back of the coins as a matter of record?

It is, of course, also possible that the cross is in reality a Chrismon, or monogram of Christ. In an article in the *Numismatic Review* of July, 1944, I discussed the subject of *graffiti* or personal inscriptions scratched onto ancient gold coins of the early Christian period. I had discovered that the Chrismon occurred more often than any other combination of letters. The Chrismon, also called Christogram, consists of the letters XP which is Greek for CH-R, the first two letters in the word Christ, or Christos.

Sometimes the loop of the P is very small and the Chrismon has the appearance of an ordinary cross. On a coin as small as the Soter Megas coins are, it would be difficult for a diemaker to outline the loop of the letter P clearly, especially if he was not a very artistic craftsman schooled in the finer work of Greek mints.

Although the Chrismon inscriptions on the coins do not go back beyond the fourth century A.D., the Chrismon itself is much older and was used simultaneously with the simple cross as a symbol identifying the object on which it appeared as *Christian.* Therefore, it is a moot question whether the horseman holds in his raised hand a cross or the monogram of Christ, for either one of these symbols denotes the same thing, Christianity as a faith and philosophy.

Dr. Gardner wrote of the strange coins: "The nameless King, who calls himself merely Soter Megas, naturally gives us no clue in his inscriptions to decide his affinities. Some of his coins are in type and style closely like those of Abdagases and he also makes use of the form ω. He must be of about the same period as that king, A.D. 30—50. His coins are found in great numbers in the Kabul valley."

The Abdagases Dr. Gardner refers to is the same nephew and co-regent of Caspar-Gondophares who went to Palestine and brought back Thomas.

But since the Soter Megas coins vary considerably in style and appearance, they may have been issued for a long time *after* the death of Caspar. Caspar-Gondophares was already king in 4 B.C., and ruled at least twenty-six years. But he may have been dead by the year 35 A.D. when these coins should be placed.

Was the deity on the front of the coins an adaptation of the Greek god Apollo, often shown surrounded by the rays of the sun? The deity holds a scepter, not a sword or lance, pointing up his peaceful intents. The fact that the animal on the backside of the coin is not always clearly recognizable as a camel shows that the artist himself never actually saw a camel. Could he have been removed by some years from the actual event? Were the Soter Megas coins started upon the death of Caspar as a tribute to both Jesus and their beloved king?

Evidently, the kingdom of Caspar-Gondophares and his family lasted for some time despite its Christian faith amid hostile nations. Parthian by race, Gondophares and his house were still flourishing thirty years later. Coins with their names were found around Kandahar, Seistan, Kabul, Peshawar, roughly today's Afghanistan.

We have the testimony of an anonymous Egyptian merchant who informs us of the existence of a Parthian realm at the mouth of the river Indus during the reign of the Roman Emperor Vespasian, 69 to 79 A.D.

The source for this statement is the so-called *Periplus maris*, quoted by the famed historian, Theodor Mommsen.

I took another look at both coins. Caspar's coins, too, show a monogram, the same royal monogram that appears also on the money of his nephew and of his brother; thus it must have some family meaning. The monogram is nothing but the astrological symbol for Mercury.

Mercury, messenger of the gods? Mercury, who brings good tidings?

Did Caspar consider himself indeed a messenger? Great emphasis is put in early Christianity on the idea of the *messenger*, both mortal and heavenly. The term "angel," derived from the Greek *angelos*, means nothing more than messenger.

I re-examined the word "theos" (God) on the coins of Soter Megas heralding the arrival of Jesus.

The monogram could also be read in a different way, with astrological meaning. The three symbols stand for Sun, Earth, Water, the three main elements of life—but fire, the fourth, is absent. Does this omission denote an early belief in hell-fire and damnation? The ancients liked to weave symbols into their art work.

Caspar's identity was assured. He really lived, he really came to Jerusalem.

10

The Identities of Melchior and Balthasar

THE OTHER two Kings, I realized, might not be so easy to pinpoint, as the areas over which they ruled were less known than India. But I had established one date, and this would be helpful in narrowing down the area, the time period, in which I was to look for them.

In archaeology we sometimes find evidence for an event in sources about an entirely *different* event, and only by using analogies do we arrive at the required proof. A contemporary writer might, for instance, mention that a certain ruler of Phoenicia visited Rome in a certain year. Then, at another time, in another manuscript, we might find reference to this ruler as being the contemporary or friend or enemy of an obscure king of Arabia about whom nothing definite had been known until now. By this indirect method we are able to date the obscure king of Arabia for the first time. Putting things together is the only way to reconstruct long-forgotten events when we don't have actual eye-witnesses or records.

For the next few months I was too preoccupied with my other work to think much about the three Kings. But they were always there, in the back of my mind.

I believe the second chapter in my search was started inadvertently when I met a young man named Melchior, whose father is a famous singer. Our meeting had nothing to do with my quest, but the name started a chain reaction which ended with my return to the files on the Wisemen.

Always in the middle, Melchior—the Wiseman, not my acquaintance—is depicted as a young man without beard. I already had a conviction that Melchior was an Arab from the city of Petra.

Professor Dalman's report on the new excavations at Petra contains a discussion of the royal house of Aretas, which ruled the Nabataean Arabs. These Arabs in what is today the Sinai Peninsula were highly civilized people with a smattering of Greek culture. They had adopted Judaism as their official religion, thereby indicating their refusal of the Roman state religion accepted by the subjugated people all around them. Prior to the coming of Jesus, there were converts to Jewish monotheism in many parts of the world. The royal house of Adiabene had turned to Judaism as had the Nabataean Arabs, whose capital city was Petra.

Both Dalman and Sir George Hill of the British Museum established the dates of rule for all of Nabataea's kings. The Great Aretas, the fourth of this name, was king from 9 B.C. to 40 A.D. Even if we allow for the generally accepted error in dating the Christian Era to the year zero, it is clear that Aretas was king of Nabataea during the entire lifespan of Jesus.

But there were several rulers named Malichus among the Nabataean kings. It is nothing more than a Latin version of the Semitic Malik, which can mean both great and king, but which is equally common as a personal name even today.

The first Nabataean ruler named Malichus ruled from 60 to 30 B.C., and was a friend and contemporary of Julius Caesar. He certainly wasn't the man. A second Malichus is placed between the years 40 and 71 A.D. This Malichus II was an ally of Vespasian, archenemy of the Palestinian Jews, according to the historian Flavius Josephus, who calls him "the Arab Malchos." Evidently his Hebrew faith did not prevent this ruler from playing politics against other Hebrews. The only other royal Malichus, if indeed there was one, came even later, and just as Malichus II, does not fit in with the time table for the Journey to Jerusalem.

But the Great Aretas did have a son named Malichus who later became king. Since Aretas ruled a long time, the second Malichus was already a middle-aged man when his father died and would not be the same young Melchior shown on all paintings of the three Wisemen.

When the other two Kings passed through Petra and invited, presumably, their host Aretas to accompany them to Jerusalem, the king knew better than to put himself into the lair of his political enemy Herod. But he might have sent young Malichus along, who could have been a brother or his son, since the Journey, in my opinion, took place in the year 5 B.C., when Aretas was only in his fifth year of reign.

Whether son or brother to Aretas, a prince of royal blood named Malichus joined the other two Wisemen in their Journey to Palestine. If it was indeed the heir presumptive Malichus, he must have been no more than fifteen years of age at the time. His portrait, showing him as king many years later, does appear on the coins of Nabataea.

There is still another reason why I think the house of Aretas was involved in the Journey of the Magi. On some of the coins issued in the name of Aretas IV, the word *shalom,* meaning "peace," appears.

Had not Jesus been called the Prince of Peace, and had not the world at this turn of events been yearning for peace, wartorn as it was all over? I was sure for the first time of the identity of two of the Wisemen. I wanted that *third man* also. This proved to be a particularly vexing pursuit.

I had little to go on, except that the third King was always shown black or dark-skinned and that he brought the Christ child myrrh. Also, as I have already mentioned, that myrrh comes from the Red Sea countries, and I knew that during the period under investigation Ethiopia ruled over portions of Arabia as well.

But where does one check into Ethiopia's ancient kings?

Again, scholars have been "at it" for over a hundred years. In 1853, Professor August Dillmann, a German archaeologist, had published the so-called *Royal Ethiopian Lists* in his *History of the Abyssinian Empire*. Some thirty years later, a Frenchman named Drouin also published these lists with critical comments, but his work is buried in a periodical called *Archaeological Review*.

According to these scholars, the early Ethiopian material is of questionable accuracy and only from about 1000 A.D. were there official chroniclers in Ethiopia. However, despite the general uncertainty of most of the records, there are two reliable documents listing Ethiopian rulers from the time of Makeda, better known as the Queen of Sheba, to the last king of the "first period," named *Beese Bazen*. Next to his name in these two lists I found a statement that reads:

"In the year eight of the reign of Bazen, Christ was born."

The documents, written about 1740, list most rulers correctly, but in some cases the chronological order may be incorrect. Still, both Dillmann and Drouin felt that the two lists from Makeda to Bazen were an exception, as many of the names checked out correctly.

Christianity had come to Ethiopia around 330 A.D. The people themselves were Kushites, that is, Semitic immigrants from Asia who had intermingled with a native African Negroid population. Thus they were generally dark-skinned and short.

When the Italians under Mussolini invaded and subjugated free Ethiopia in 1936, the more modern methods of Italian scientists followed the invading armies into Africa. Thus, new evidence was unearthed about the dim past of the country. Excavations started shortly after the 1936 invasion and reported in the journal of the Italian Archaeological Institute shed further light on the period of Beese Bazen.

Sometimes spelled Bizi Bazen, the word Bizi was said to be a Greek transcription of the native Ethiopian word Beesey, meaning "Man from."

Was this true?

I examined some of the rare Axumite coins of ancient and medieval Ethiopia—Axum was then the capital—and found that the term frequently appears on them. Usually it is followed by a locality name, such as Bizi Dachy, Bizi Dimele, Bizi Gisene. Bizi Bazen means "the Man from Bazen." But Bizi can also be followed by a tribal or family name, very much like our "of" or the German "von."

Eastern traditions always stress the tribal name rather than a first or given name. Ben Akiba and Ibn Sa'ud are examples of this method.

How did Beese (or Bizi) Bazen become Balthasar?

To the Syrian Christians, who had but recently relinquished their heathen god Bal, the dark skin of the third Wiseman suggested their Bal or Belzebub, which now had turned from a local Phoenician deity into the devil. The old forms of the name, Beltesan and Belzesan, also exist, showing how the name Beese Bazen gradually became Balthazar.

Capernaum

I checked on the interpretation Professors Drouin and Dillmann gave for the meaning of the word Beese. Drouin translated it as "courageous," and Dillmann called it "warrior." I simply called it "Man from," but I don't think I am in conflict with these two interpretations. An Ethiopian in ancient times had to be courageous, and a warrior, if he was to be considered a man.

The amazing thing about the discovery and pinpointing of the identity of the third Wiseman was that it matched so tenuous a fact as tradition: the third Wiseman, Balthasar, was indeed dark-skinned.

But in showing that the dark-skinned Wiseman was the ruler of Ethiopia, I had also demolished any fanciful notions that three Persians had come to call on the Christ child. How anyone claiming them to have been from one country and background could have gotten over the glaring differences in their appearances in all representations, whether in words or in pictures, is hard to understand.

Interesting, too, is the fact that to this very day the descendants of these very men rule the countries whence they came. Northwestern India is still largely populated by the Aryan Hindus, the Nabataean desert still belongs to the Arabs, and the Emperor of Ethiopia is still a dark-skinned man.

Perhaps that, too, is as it should be.

The Journey of the Wisemen was more than an episode in Biblical history. It is a journey that men are still making every day of their lives, a search for the light that will lead them out of the darkness of their baser instincts.

11

The True Meaning of Christmas

I BECAME elated and calm at the same time. It was near Christmas again and in my heart I felt that I had earned a specially good Christmas this year.

Caspar, Melchior, and Balthasar were no longer colorful symbols in a book called the Bible, nor figments of anyone's imagination. They were actual people who lived and died in the first century of our era.

In the process of corroborating the evidence for the existence of the three Wisemen, I had also suggested that many passages in our everyday version of the Bible needed new readings. Was this harmful to religion?

Not at all.

If religion is something more than a blind adherence to a fixed faith because of social, economic, or family pressure, then it thrives on new readings. The living religion need not fear one iota will ever be taken from it.

Although it seems scientifically certain that Jesus the Christ was not born on December 25, year zero—or any other December 25, for that matter—but several years prior and at a different time of year at that, in no way does it change *the meaning of Christmas.*

As we have seen, the festival celebrated by the Christian world on December 25 of our current calendar is merely a takeover of a much older ritual celebrated to mark the winter solstice. It was at that time that man would look inside himself for a guiding thought, to take stock of his life in the past year, and to plan ahead for the next. It was a time, too, when man should think kindly of his fellow man, and take him to his heart merely because he was a fellow man.

The expression "Love thy neighbor as thyself" is older than Christianity, coming of course from Hebrew traditions. Love indeed is the key word to spirituality, a positive vibration set up emotionally and in thought toward the world around us.

It does not seem to work at present. But it may work someday, if enough human beings will continue to practice what is the only true spirit of the original Christmas.

The three Wisemen came to Jerusalem out of curi-

Nazareth

osity, but they left with a sense of fulfillment.

Three contemporaries of Jesus have stepped forth from the pages of the Bible into a tangible archaeological world. Through them the unusual circumstances surrounding the birth of Jesus become at once real and immediate, and like the Wisemen two thousand years ago, we too may follow the *Star in the East.*

Format by Ellen H. Brecher
Set in Caslon
Composed, printed and bound by The Haddon Craftsmen, Inc.
HARPER & ROW, PUBLISHERS, INCORPORATED